**by Piera Paltro**

# Our Father

Illustrated by
Anna Maria Curti

**Pauline**
**BOOKS & MEDIA**
BOSTON

Translated by
Daughters of St. Paul

# Our Father

My daddy is not
Ronnie's daddy,
and he's not Debbie's
daddy, either.
Some children do not
even have a father.
And not all fathers are
as good
as we would like them
to be.

But instead, dear God,
you are my Father,
and Ronnie's Father,
and Debbie's Father.
You are everyone's
Father no matter who
they are.

You are good.
You are great!
No one can say,
"God is my Father.
and nobody else's."
We all say together:
"God is OUR good Father."
It's really beautiful!

We are all brothers
and sisters.

Wouldn't it be great if all
five billion people
on this earth
would cry out together:

# Our Father

# ...who art in heaven

The heavens are so beautiful,
Father!
From here I can only
see the part around
the North Star.
Other children live where
they can only see the
part around Sirius,
the brightest star in the whole sky...

But *your* heavens are
something different.
They are your home.
You are in the North,
the South, and
everywhere.
We don't have to travel
to reach your heavens.

We come to you by
loving you and by
loving each other.
I wonder how many
people are already
in your house!
I think about this
when I say:
OUR FATHER

# who art in heaven

# hallowed be thy name

Father, I already know a lot of people by name... Mom, Dad, and many others. I know people on radio and television, and in the comics. Then I'll learn about a lot more in school — kings and presidents, scientists and heroes....

But your name
is the most
wonderful of all.
It means that
you are with us
and that you are good;
that you can do everything,
and that you love us very much.

I will never forget this!
I wish that everyone would know
you are God, and so I will
pray every day:

## hallowed be thy name.

# thy kingdom come

Father, I am not always
obedient, and sometimes
not even very honest,
but I do like to be happy.
It would be wonderful if no
one ever quarreled
and there were no
robbers or criminals.

I know that if we would all
obey you and Jesus, who
came to teach us how
to be good,

the whole world would become
such a beautiful place!

No more lies, no more evil,
no more robbers or criminals.
Then no one would cry anymore.
It would be almost like
the kingdom that Jesus
has prepared for those
who are good.
I want this to happen, so
every day I ask you:

**thy kingdom come**

# thy will
# be done

Father, I know
that police arrest
robbers and
put them in jail
because they have
disobeyed the law.
Every country on the earth
has laws so its people can
live together in peace.

Father, your law
is best of all!
You first gave it to
your friend Moses
and then your
son Jesus came
to explain it
to us even more.
You are good and
your law, which is
your will, is good, too.
I will always
trust you and say:

**thy will
be done.**

# on earth as
# it is in heaven

In your house, Father,
everyone is happy.
With you no one is sad
or mean or selfish.
The people who are
in your house
were good on earth.

Now we must follow
their example.
Help me to remember
this when I want
to fight or talk back
or when I don't want
to pray or be kind.

Please help me to
remember that
I should try to please you.
So I won't forget,
I will repeat every day:
thy will be done

# on earth as it is in heaven.

# Give us this day our daily bread

Father, I like many things.
I like candy and toys and
flowers and my home...
and a lot of other things, too.
If my mother does not give me
what I want I get upset.

But when my mother is sick or
my father is tired, I know getting
upset doesn't help at all.
I know that if you do not help us,
Father, no one else can make the sun

shine or give us fresh air,
good health, or life.

I know that if important
things like bread are missing,
it is because we do not
care for each other's
needs as you want us to.
But you are always ready
to listen to us.
So I say to you:

# Give us this day our daily bread

# and forgive us our trespasses...

I've seen signs that say
NO TRESPASSING.
Those signs mean:
"This property belongs to
someone, so don't come near it."

When we say,
"forgive us our trespasses,"
we mean forgive us
for the times when
we were careless about
the feelings of others;
when we hurt them or
made them upset.
One time I upset my mother
and I knew I had to
ask forgiveness because
this was a debt not of money
but of love.

Father,
you want the best
for us, and you
teach us to
always try our best.
I know that I disobey
you when I am mean
or selfish or naughty—
it's like trespassing
where I don't belong.
I'm really sorry that
I do these things,
and so I say for myself
and for everyone...

**forgive us
our trespasses...**

# as we forgive those who trespass against us

The other day,
Father,
I was not very good.
One of my friends
punched me once,
so I hit him back
three times.
Many people argue
and fight.
But I know that
getting even
is not right,
no matter what!

I want you to always
forgive me when I ask.
So if somebody hurts
me and then asks
for forgiveness,
I can't say:
"I'm not that dumb!"
I will say: "Yes" and
try to really mean it.
I know this will please you.
Then I can say:

## as we forgive those who trespass against us.

# and lead us not into temptation

A temptation
is when somebody
wants to tell lies, or
disobey, or steal,
even though this
will not please you.
I wonder why being bad
often seems so good?
I feel this way sometimes,
but I know it is wrong.

It's really not nice
when we know
that you want us to
do one thing and
we do something else.
Do you know what I mean?

I think it is hard to
be always good like you,
but I want to try.
I know you will
always help me,
so I will keep asking you:

# lead us not into temptation

# but deliver us from evil

I would like to be a fireman
who rescues people from burning
buildings, or a sheriff who
saves people from bandits.
You know what, Father?
I would like to get there
just in time and say:
"Here I am! You're safe!"

Jesus warned us that the
real enemy is EVIL.

This enemy can make
us feel like doing
what is wrong.
(Cain proved this
when he killed
his brother Abel.
Judas proved it when
he betrayed Jesus.)
Father, protect us from evil.
You can really say:
"Look! I am here. You are safe!"
I will remind you every day:

# but deliver us
# from evil

So now with all my heart I can say:

**"Our Father, who art in heaven,**
**hallowed be thy name;**
**thy kingdom come;**
**thy will be done on earth**
**as it is in heaven.**
**Give us this day our daily bread;**
**and forgive us our trespasses**
**as we forgive those who trespass against us;**
**and lead us not into temptation,**
**but deliver us from evil. Amen."**

I can say it with all my heart
and it seems to me that
now I really understand
what I am saying.
I feel sure I will always
say this prayer, even
when I am grown up
like Dad,
and when I get old
like Grandpa...
always, Father.